Happy Tails

I would like to thank all the cats and kittens who contributed to this book. I also thank those humans who opened their hearts and adopted these precious babies. A big *mahalo* to the amazing staff at the Kauai Humane Society as well. And a very special thank-you to cat whisperer Neil Rice. A portion of the proceeds from the sales of this book will be donated to the Kauai Humane Society.

Note: Some of the cats' names and details have been changed to protect their privacy. To the best of my knowledge, every cat depicted in this book has found a loving home.

ISBN: 978-1-68088-502-6

◗ and Blue Mountain Press are registered in U.S. Patent and Trademark Office. Certain trademarks are used under license.

Printed in China.
First Printing: 2023

♲ This book is printed on recycled paper.

This book is printed on paper that has been specially produced to be acid free (neutral pH) and contains no groundwood or unbleached pulp. It conforms with the requirements of the American National Standards Institute, Inc., so as to ensure that this book will last and be enjoyed by future generations.

Blue Mountain Arts, Inc.
P.O. Box 4549, Boulder, Colorado 80306

Happy Tails

Life Lessons from Rescued Cats & Kittens

Jason Blume

Blue Mountain Press™
Boulder, Colorado

Introduction

I was eight years old and heartbroken when Dinky, my little black kitten, ran away. I searched the neighborhood and tacked "Lost Kitten" posters on trees and attached them to shop windows. Two days later, someone called to say he believed he had Dinky in his home—a few blocks away from mine.

When my mother and I entered the house, I saw more than twenty cats perched shoulder to shoulder on two sofas. At least a dozen cats slept on overstuffed chairs and in cardboard boxes strewn on the floor, while several big orange ones peered down from atop the refrigerator. Several kittens rubbed against my legs and meowed for attention. The man told us he was caring for forty-two formerly stray cats, and sure enough, my sweet Dinky was one of them.

That was the day I decided I wanted to be a Crazy Cat Man when I grew up. Since then, I have photographed more than 2,500 cats for my local humane society's website and provided "Pet of the Week" photos for the local newspaper. I've fostered forty neonatal kittens—bottle-feeding them every three hours throughout the night—and I feed a colony of stray and feral cats twice a day.

I never stop being inspired by these cats. They have taught me about trust, friendship, resilience, love, and so much more. My hope is that through this book I can share the gifts they have given me, the lessons they have taught me, and the joy they continue to bring me every day.

— Jason Blume

Embrace
New Beginnings

Graycie

When I began fostering Graycie, she was a frail two-week-old with a severe eye infection. I didn't know if she would make it—and if she did, would she be blind?

I gave her extra love and care, and after administering her medicines, I wrapped her in a blanket and let her sleep in my arms. As she recovered, we forged an exceptional bond.

When it was time to deliver Graycie to her new owner, I was thrilled that she would have a *furrever* home, but I grieved the loss of this sweet baby.

It is impossible for me to give foster kittens the love and the care they need without becoming deeply emotionally attached. Every time I say goodbye to one of those sweet babies, a piece of my heart goes with them—and a part of them stays with me.

In time, the empty place in my heart becomes filled with cherished memories and the satisfaction that comes with knowing they have found the loving homes they deserve.

To embark on a new chapter, we must turn the page on the past.

Celebrate What Makes You Unique

Bowie

Bowie, with his two different-colored eyes, was a star at the shelter. People were drawn to his unusual looks, and he was adopted within a few days of his arrival.

Those things that make each of us special are precious. There is no one else quite like you in the whole world. Celebrate all that is unique about you. No one has ever risen to the top by being just like everyone else.

Embrace your differences. You're the cat's meow!

Be your own one-of-a-kind beautiful.

Live in the Moment

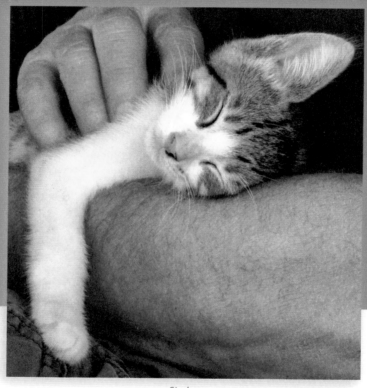

Simba

When Simba stretches out on a cushion in a warm, sunny spot, he is the very picture of peace and serenity. He needs nothing more than the warmth and sunshine to bask in that perfect moment.

Cats live fully in the now, not worrying about what tomorrow might bring. They do not place conditions on their happiness, such as "I will be okay… when I have more money, when I lose weight, when I retire, when I find the perfect relationship, or when the children are older."

Everything does not need to be right in our worlds for us to be happy.

The time to enjoy and appreciate life is now.

Stay Curious

Leilani

For cats, adventure awaits around every corner. Each nook and cranny provide a new, exciting opportunity for exploration.

Watching kittens investigate their world can remind us to seek out our own novel experiences.

Learning a new skill, visiting a place we've never been, listening to new music, trying a new recipe, and meeting new people adds richness to our lives and helps us stay sharp and vital.

Remain open to new experiences.

Enjoy Life's Simple Pleasures

Roscoe

Cats don't need expensive toys to have fun. They can entertain themselves for hours with a feather, a shoestring, a paper bag, or a cardboard box.

We humans sometimes think material things such as fancy cars, a big house, the latest electronic gadgets, and money in the bank hold the keys to happiness. But a summer sunset, a walk in the woods, a favorite piece of music, a stroll in a garden, and sharing laughter with friends can fill our hearts with smiles—and they don't cost a thing.

Seek out those everyday things that make you happy.

Look for the
Silver Lining

Lily

When Lily and her four littermates were approximately one week old, they were found beside a dumpster in a cardboard box and were brought to the humane society.

It broke my heart that such young kittens were deprived of their mother. Traps were set in hopes that their mother would return—but she did not. I thought life had dealt these tiny kittens the cruelest blow.

I fostered the babies, bottle-feeding them and showering them with love and affection. They became the most affectionate kittens I had ever fostered.

When they were old enough to be adopted, these little angels went to loving *purrmanent* homes.

Had they not been separated from their mother, they would have likely lived as feral cats, foraging for food and never knowing the love of humans.

Lily (six weeks old)

Sometimes, what we think is the worst thing turns out to be the best.

Convey Your Contentment

Harry

Cats purr when they are content. That soft vibration tells us they are happy.

A cat's purr can melt our hearts. It lets us know we are doing something right—that we are being appreciated.

We can let others know we are pleased by sharing a smile, a gentle touch, a kind word, or a thank-you.

**Find your own
ways to purr.**

Find Comfort in Friendship

Bunny and Mango

Bunny was found at a recycling center. She was terribly thin and had injured one of her paws. When she arrived at the shelter, she hid, trembling with fear, in a box at the back of her cage.

A few days later, Mango was left in a crate outside the humane society—and Bunny had a roommate.

At first they growled, hissed, and swatted as they staked out their territories, unsure if they could trust each other. But soon they were playing together, cuddling, grooming each other, and sleeping together. They became the best of friends, finding comfort in being together.

When someone came to adopt Mango, it was plain to see that these two kittens were inseparable.

The two best friends were adopted together.

Friends make life
so much sweeter.

Be of
Service

Mitzi

Many of the kittens brought to my local humane society are the offspring of feral cats. When I foster these babies, I know I am changing their lives.

By holding and cuddling them, bottle-feeding and playing with them, I am training them to be comfortable with humans. I am teaching them to be loving companions.

When these kittens are adopted and go to their new homes, they become part of a family, sharing love and earning a place in beautiful memories.

By giving kittens a loving start, I am not only changing the lives of those kittens and of the families that adopt them. I am changing my own.

The deepest rewards come from helping others.

Make Time
to Play

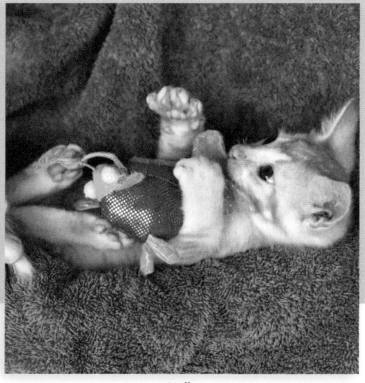

Muffin

Kittens play with complete abandon, lost in the moment without a care in the world. Watching them bat a ball, chase a ribbon, or pounce on a catnip mouse, I am reminded to carve time out of my schedule to do the things that bring me pleasure.

Whether we play with a kitten, play a game with a friend, pursue a craft, or participate in a sport, taking a break and having fun reduces stress and makes us more productive.

Life is meant to be enjoyed.

Listen to Your Body

Pumpkin

When kittens get tired, they rest. They don't push themselves to lick their paws, sharpen their claws, or attend to the myriad of other tasks kittens need to do. When they get sleepy, they find a comfy spot and take a time-out.

We humans press ourselves from one project to the next in an effort to accomplish a never-ending to-do list. Get plenty of rest, take catnaps, exercise, and eat well. You might be amazed at how much more you can get done—and how much better you feel.

Let your body tell you what it needs.

Express
Your Needs

Celine

When one of my cats wants something, it lets me know with a loud meow, a tap with its paw, a gentle nip, or by rubbing against my leg.

I never need to worry about forgetting when it's time to feed my cats their afternoon treats or when it is their evening playtime. I get loud, insistent reminders.

Sometimes we expect those around us to read our minds and know what we want from them. Asking for what we want can be tough, because we run the risk of being rejected. But unexpressed expectations are resentments waiting to happen.

Let others know what you would like from them.

Learn to Trust

Moo-Moo

Moo-Moo had a rough start to her life. She was approximately six weeks old when a family noticed a group of teenagers at a beach park taunting her and pulling her tail. They brought Moo-Moo home, planning to take her to the humane society.

One week later, I met them at a store where they were buying food and supplies for the tiny kitten that they had decided to keep.

Moo-Moo had spent three days hiding under a bed, trembling. She flinched and hissed when they tried to pet her. The family reassured her with gentle words. They left her food at the edge of the bed and placed a litterbox nearby.

With time and patience, the kitten learned she was safe with these people. Soon, she purred when they petted her. Before long, she was following them from room to room and sleeping cuddled against them.

She learned to love—and be loved.

We can learn to trust again.
Never stop believing in happy endings.

Believe in the Power
of Unconditional Love

Leonardo

Cats don't judge us by our accomplishments, by our successes, or by what we think of as our failures.

The love they give us is not based on our social standing, our appearance, our finances, or our jobs.

Cats only require kindness to reward us with their affection. Their love is pure. It soothes and comforts us. They accept us for who we are.

Loving and being loved—without conditions—are the greatest gifts we can give and receive.

Accept Yourself...
Flaws and All

Molly

Molly was seven years old when her owners left her at the shelter. They were moving away and couldn't take Molly with them.

Days turned into weeks and weeks turned into months while potential adopters passed her over. They chose cats that were younger or ones with silkier fur and prettier coats.

Then a kind young man stopped at her cage and slid his hand through the bars. Molly pressed her face against his fingers and purred. The man opened his heart and brought Molly home.

He stroked her fur, petted her, hugged her, and told her she was loved—and that she was beautiful. His eyes saw through to Molly's heart, and all he could see was *purrfection*. As she gazed up at him, it was clear she felt the same way about her new best friend.

Accept yourself—and others—"as is."
It's nice not needing to be *purrfect*.

Make Your Own Good Luck

Shoyu

Shoyu was the most affectionate and playful kitten in his litter. But he came to the humane society with two strikes against him: the shelter already had an abundance of black kittens, and because of the myth about black cats being bad luck, it is especially challenging to find homes for them.

A potential adopter browsing through the photos at the shelter's website requested to meet Shoyu's sister. A stunningly beautiful gray tabby, I knew she would have no trouble finding a home.

I brought Shoyu along, hoping the woman might take both of them, but she said she could only take one.

As they spent time together, Shoyu charmed the adopter, nuzzling against her neck, batting at her earrings, and purring as she stroked his face. He beat the odds and won her heart—and a forever home—with his exceptional *purrsonality*.

We cannot change the circumstances we are born into, but the choices we make and the actions we take can create our best future.

Shine

Blaze

When Blaze was brought to the shelter, it was immediately apparent that he was an exceptional kitten. He would rush to the front of his cage, standing on his hind legs, meowing, and demanding attention from any potential adopter. It was impossible to pass by him without smiling.

We receive so many messages telling us not to stand out: Be modest. Don't be a showoff. Don't draw attention to yourself. Blend in with the crowd. But you are an amazing person. Be proud of your accomplishments. Share your gifts and your talents. Be the light in the darkness, the hope in the sadness, and the encouraging smile in a world that needs love.

Be all you were born to be.

About the Author

Award-winning photographer Jason Blume travels the world teaching songwriting master classes, delivering motivational keynote speeches, and taking photographs of the animals and landscapes that never cease to inspire him. He is a hit songwriter and author of three best-selling books on songwriting. Jason's songs have sold more than fifty million copies and have been recorded by artists ranging from Britney Spears and the Backstreet Boys to country stars Collin Raye, John Berry, and the Oak Ridge Boys. His writing is featured on Blue Mountain Arts greeting cards, books, and calendars that have sold more than seven million copies.

To learn more about Jason Blume, visit his website, www.jasonblume.com.